Renewed Soul

Finding a New Meaning in Life

Blanca Gatica

© Copyright 2024 ISBN: 9798328139441

Dedication:

To all souls who feel lonely and empty, and to those who have lost their sense of living."

Gratitude:

To the team of Master Francisco Navarro Lara, for sharing their knowledge and guiding me on the path to achieve this goal. To Elizabeth Pérez, loyal friend, and to my sister Rosita for the feedback and time dedicated to reviewing the essays in this book. To Gabriel Escobar, for his valuable professional comments. To all the people whose stories helped inspire this narrative. To you, the reader, for the time you dedicate to this story."

INDEX:

PREFACE

INTRODUCTION

PART ONE

    CHAPTER ONE

    A Love Story and Redemption

    SIMONA – Another Lesson on Forgiveness

    CHAPTER TWO

    The Seed of Success

PART TWO

    CHAPTER THREE

    Taking Risks and Overcoming Obstacles

PART THREE

    CHAPTER FOUR

    The Transition

    CHAPTER FIVE

    Finding a New Meaning in Life

CHAPTER SIX

Embracing Uncertainty

CHAPTER SEVEN

The Revelation and Rebirth

EPILOGUE

To laugh often and much; to win the respect of intelligent people and the affection of children; to earn the appreciation of honest critics; to endure the betrayal of false friends; to appreciate beauty; to find the best in others; to leave the world a bit better, whether by a healthy child, a garden patch, or a redeemed social condition; to know that one life has breathed easier because you lived. This is to have succeeded." – Ralph Waldo Emerson

FOREWORD

Welcome to a journey that goes beyond the written pages. This book seeks not only to be read but felt in the depths of the soul. The motivation that drove me to write these lines arises from the genuine desire to leave a legacy, to share the lessons that life has taught me along my journey, and to bring a touch of hope to those who feel they have lost the guiding light in their lives. Within these pages, you will not only find my experiences and personal memories with a touch of fiction but also the influence of real-life characters who have left an indelible mark on my path.

In certain segments of this novel, my inspiration is drawn from the work of Dr. Viktor Frankl, an Austrian psychologist and Holocaust survivor. His lessons on finding meaning amidst adversity resonated deeply within me, guiding me in the exploration of my own existence and purpose, especially in the golden stage of my life.

I hope this book not only provides you with knowledge but also inspiration and comfort in moments of doubt, emptiness, and tribulation. May you find within these pages the strength to face your own challenges and the clarity to discover your own path to personal fulfillment.

Thank you for joining me on this journey of self-discovery and growth. May our shared experiences illuminate our way toward a fuller and more meaningful life.

Let's go, the journey begins now!

INTRODUCTION:

Through the experience of the main protagonist, Mónica Villarreal, and important characters in the story's development, such as her parents, her grandmother, and some "angels", unfolds a tale of love, redemption, and goal achievement in Mónica's quest for the meaning of life. Developed between the post- II World War era and the present decade, the setting spans between Guatemala and the United States. This narrative reveals how the fulfillment of goals and the achievement of success have been fundamental pillars in giving meaning to the main protagonist's life. The early chapters describe Mónica's beginnings, adolescence, and early youth to provide context; in the later chapters of this novel, she describes the challenges of reaching the golden age and retirement stage and the challenges it presents. In the final stage of the narration, it describes how upon reaching retirement, Mónica feels the need to reassess and find new horizons that provide a renewed purpose. This process of reflection and search becomes a journey towards self-realization and fulfillment. The narrative at times highlights how the achievement of personal goals can give meaning to life even in the darkest and most confusing moments.

This work not only offers us an intimate look into the life of the main protagonist, Mónica Villarreal, but also provides valuable advice for charting our own path towards goal achievement and personal fulfillment. Through these pages, we are reminded of the importance of pursuing our dreams and aspirations, as they are what truly give meaning to life.

This work is narrated in three parts: childhood and adolescence; adulthood and professional life, and finally, the golden years and retirement as a single woman. Some character names may have been changed to maintain the privacy of the individuals involved.

PART ONE

-"He who has a 'why' to live can bear almost any 'how'."

-"Love is the primary and highest goal which a man can aspire." -

Viktor Frankl

CHAPTER ONE

A Story of Love and Redemption

On an April afternoon, seated on a bench in the central park of Antigua Guatemala, located 40 kilometers from the capital of Guatemala, we find Mónica Villarreal, her daughter Génesis, and their close friend Patty. Enjoying the peace brought by the scent of 'floripondio,' the local flower known for its sedative and relaxing properties, the three of them relish the scene before them: a fountain surrounded by flowers, the colonial-style cathedral, and indigenous women selling their colorful textiles. Mónica feels inspired and thinks it's the opportune moment to initiate a conversation she has long wanted to have with Génesis. Patty occasionally chimes in.

Mónica:

"Come, Génesis, child of my heart. I want to tell you a bit about our family and my story. Let's embark on this journey of introspection to share lessons learned during my time on this earth.

I called the first stage of my childhood "A Gift to My Sister" because I was born on the day my sister turned three, on a hot August day, in a lower-middle-class neighborhood in Guatemala City. My parents organized a birthday party for my sister Anita. Several family members arrived, and it was also the baptism of my brother Julián, who was barely a year old. My dad took a photo where my mom is hiding because, being pregnant, she didn't want to be in the picture; obviously, her huge belly was noticeable. In the photo, you can see her profile. That photo was taken at two in the afternoon, and I was born at seven in the evening. So, I was a gift for my sister, ha, ha, ha! I like to see it that way. To this day, I have a very lovely relationship with her. From childhood, I realized that she was also a gift to me.

That day was the day after Marilyn Monroe's death. So, I like to think that she was going up, and I was coming down, ha, ha, ha! I like to imagine she must have said something good to me in that encounter halfway. You know, a bit of wisdom, because even though her reputation was dubious, she knew how to navigate the high circles of her time, and although she left very young, she managed to achieve many of her dreams.

Génesis:

"Oh, how wonderful, Mom! Tell me more... what was lifelike in your home during that time?"

Mónica:

My mom was my dad's second significant relationship, although initially, she didn't know about his previous partner. I was the fourth child of both, and in the end, they had six children (Rubén, Anita, Julián, Me, Tati, and José), although my dad had a total of 15 children.

As I mentioned before, I always had a good relationship with my sister Anita. With my brother Rubén, my parents' first child, I had a somewhat distant relationship because he was imposing being older, and he left home very early. I have a lot to thank him for because he was the one who checked my homework in elementary school, and in adolescence, he taught me how to drive. Besides, he has always been there for me when I needed him, just like my other siblings whose names I mentioned above; I have always received unconditional love from them. My parents never checked my schoolwork; they were too busy working. My dad was a carpenter and had several furniture stores; besides, they were building a cinema, the new family business. My mom helped him in all aspects; she also ran a bakery of which they were also owners.

We grew up with the idea of work, work, work, and I never saw my parents take time off, except for my dad, who took a 15-minute nap every day. I vividly remember my dad having breakfast and lunch with us, but he never had dinner with us; he always went to see his other children, my half-siblings. That was his way of being a responsible father. My mom was always very generous; every day, without my dad asking, she would go out to say goodbye to him at the door with a sack full of bread, and it was my job to make sure my dad took that bag full of bread every day for his other children; something I didn't see them to appreciate in my childhood. Sometimes I had to run after him or go in a public bus with my brother Rubén to the other "kids' house" to deliver the bag full of bread. At that time, parents sent you in a bus, public transportation, alone at 5 to 7 years old. For example, my brother Rubén would go to the "terminal" (a mega-market of all kinds of products) to do the shopping at 7 years old, a child, alone, on a public bus!... Those were different times when people didn't know as much about human malice and cruelty.

My dad was a very entrepreneurial man who only completed third grade, very skilled in business, and because of those qualities, the ladies followed him; a slip with his secretary became his third significant relationship. I say significant because she gave him three children, not because he loved her, only he knew that - he took that to his grave because he never actually left my mom, and I always had a kiss from him before going to sleep. A carpenter by trade, he started young. At 19, he already had his own carpentry workshop, without having finished elementary school; he went on to have three furniture stores and a cinema in Guatemala City! In their lives, they were both very entrepreneurial; they had various types of businesses with my mom, from the bakery, the cinema, the carpentry workshop, fashion workshop, egg sales, grocery store, car importation, shares in public transportation, aluminum, and glass importation, etc. They never rested. Not bad for someone who didn't finish elementary school; they were quite successful materially, and although many of those businesses failed, they always kept going.

My mom left her home at around 15 years old to work as a domestic worker. My grandmother used to collect her salary every month. In that job, my mom learned to make cakes and poundcakes, which later became very popular and helped contribute to the household economy. When she found out she was pregnant with her first child, she told her employer, where she also lived, that the last two months' salary should be given to her because she didn't have a penny, not to my grandmother because she would need that money to cover the baby's needs. So, my mom decided not to move in with her parents; she was going to have her baby while working with her or was going to find a new place to live alone. The employer cared for her and paid her directly, so my grandmother got angry because she wouldn't have that salary at her disposal anymore. Nowadays, we would call it economic abuse.

My Parents met when she was about 17 years old, and he must have been around 25. They met at a party; that's all I know because they never wanted to talk much about their relationship. They were very private, and everything related to sex was a taboo, to the point that I never saw them kiss. To this day, I think I inherited a certain shame about showing affection in public.

As for my dad, his way of expressing affection to my mom was to stroke her arm or pass by and give her a playful slap on the buttocks, ha, ha, ha! She would just say "Don Jorge!" very surprised and embarrassed. He would say "Doña Con" because her full name was Consuelo, so that's how they addressed each other. They slept in separate beds, thank goodness! in the same room but separate, and thank goodness it was like that because otherwise, how many children would we have been! Ha, ha, ha!

My dad was a charmer; he liked leather jackets; he liked the "James Dean" style. He rode one of those big motorcycles, like the German ones from World War II, that you could be heard from two blocks away. Plus, he had a very special charisma; he was quite sociable with people he liked because if he didn't like you, it was better not to get close.

As far as I know, my mom told me (when I was old enough), she didn't know that my dad had been in a relationship with someone else and already had five or six children.

She found out because his sister-in-law told her, "Jorge is married and has children."

The day my mom found out that my dad was engaged, that day she went into labor due to the emotional shock. She had my oldest brother at the Roosevelt Hospital in Guatemala City, which was newly inaugurated, in February 1956. She went to the hospital alone, and when my dad arrived at the hospital, my mom asked him, "Is it true that you're married and have children?" He said it was true... She was terribly angry!!

Later I found out - not from my dad because he never talked about his other relationships - that the reason was that his first wife had left him, that the lady always told him that he was ugly and that he was useless. A form of reverse psychological abuse. My mom, perhaps because she knew my dad wasn't entirely hers, decided to find a way to provide for herself.

Mom became independent when she had one child, at 18 years old. Their romantic relationship was unstable. She went to live in the San Antonio neighborhood in Zone 6 of Guatemala City, near the Belize Bridge. I don't know how she managed to survive, but from the comings and goings of my dad to see his new child, she became pregnant again, this time with my sister Anita. So that's when my dad decided to take the next step and move in with her because his other relationship was not going well. I remember my mom told me she used to see dad's oldest son, my eldest half-brother, used to follow my dad around with a basket, and she realized that the child/teenager had to make sure my dad filled the basket with food every day.

I always wondered why my mom forgave and endured that situation with my dad. When I started to realize their lifestyle, at 6 or 7 years old, I didn't hate my dad, not at all! I wondered how my mom could be so foolish. Even without knowledge of moral values or religion, I already knew that it wasn't right, that my dad was with us 90% of the time but the other 10% was with my half-siblings. How could she tolerate him going to dinner with his other children and seeing the other lady? Because she eventually came back when she realized he already had a relationship with mom, the lady probably wanted to secure some kind of inheritance for her children... it worked.

Said lady didn't do anything to me; rather, my mom might have done it to her, looking at it from the outside. God will be the judge. All of that prevented me from having a completely assembled family. On the other side of the world, this lifestyle was probably normal, and in Guatemala, it also seemed normal at that time. Now we would judge it with different lenses.

My dad lived to work; he was an excellent provider, we never lacked anything. Although he never bought anything for himself, and we never went on vacations anywhere, our vacations were going to visit the Esquipulas Church (on the border with El Salvador and Honduras) for a couple of days.

Génesis:

What's the happiest memory you have from your childhood? And what's the saddest memory?

Mónica:

The happiest memory I have is riding in the car with my parents, my dad driving, my mom beside him, and me hugging him from behind. I was in the back seat, hugging and kissing him because nobody in life gave me more of a sense of security than he did. He may have been whatever he was as a husband; perhaps he was very weak to the temptations of the flesh, but he always made me feel safe and always treated me like a queen. That's why I can't let a man treat me badly now. My dad taught me how a woman should be treated, even though he may not have treated his women that same way.

Other unforgettable moments were when he took us to eat "mixtas" (our version of hot dogs) to a café called "Frankfurt" on Sixth Avenue in Zone 1 of the capital in Guatemala. After spending time looking at toy stores all along Sixth Avenue, when the downtown area was safe; after dinner, he would take us to a children's playground on Las Americas Avenue, one of the few places prepared for children's entertainment. Guatemala has always had this urban problem of few recreational parks. This happened every Tuesday or Wednesday because by then the cinema was already operating, and weekends were super busy, and there was no time for outings because all the children worked at the cinema as soon as we were old enough.

I think my dad was a very visionary man. As I said, he took many risks. However, what he didn't have was a good eye for the location of the cinema. The idea was good, but Zone 6 of the capital was not a suitable neighborhood for a cinema or theater, so, as real estate experts say, in this business, everything is: Location, Location, Location. If the cinema had been on Sixth Avenue, in Zone 10, or on Roosevelt Street in the capital, it would have been another story. At that time, in the 1970s, television also started to be popular in Guatemala. Everyone wanted to have a television, so cinema sales declined, and the cinema went bankrupt. It went bankrupt because, in addition to the low attendance, my dad took out a loan of Q7000 for improvements, imagine that now it's $1000, a fortune at that time, which he couldn't pay back, and he lost the property.

Génesis: And what events impacted your life during childhood?

Mónica: The saddest and most impactful memory I have from my childhood is when I saw my dad hit my mom, forgive me if I get emotional... I don't know why they were arguing... I must have been about five years old. I saw the scene; I saw my mom fall onto a big basket of laundry clothes. She couldn't get up because it was a big, deep basket, but she didn't just stay there in the basket because she couldn't find the strength, but because she was so hurt and humiliated that all she could do was cry, and the crying wouldn't let her move. When you cry, you can't do anything else. That day, at five years old, I made a promise to myself: "I will never let a man treat me like that, and I will never cry for anyone like my mom is crying." I remember telling my dad, "Don't hit my mom!" I was furious. That's when my dad reacted, he realized he had witnesses, and I sensed that he felt bad. It was the only time I saw that kind of violence. The term "Domestic Violence" did not exist in the 1960s. After that scene, I never saw him treat her badly again, although once was enough to change my life. Sometimes, if he was in a bad mood, he spoke to her a bit harshly, but I never saw him hit her again. I think my mom had a great wisdom in knowing how to handle her situation because what I do remember is wondering how, with so many children, my parents managed to raise us because we never went hungry, we always had our own house, we had education guaranteed up to high school, we always had a toy at Christmas.

Another sad memory that taught me a lot about strength in difficult times was when I was about 12 years old. My mom went to talk to the loan shark who had lent money to my dad, and because of which we lost the cinema. She begged him, crying, to please not execute the deeds, that we would pay him but to give us time, and the loan shark treated her very badly. He said, "Those are your husband's matters, ma'am, why did he commit if he couldn't pay?" The next day, there was a foreclosure announcement in "Prensa Libre" (local newspaper) stating that the property was being in foreclosure. It was one of the first lessons my dad gave me. My mom said to him, "Did you see the announcement in "Prensa Libre" about the cinema foreclosure?", she was very embarrassed because the ladies from the neighborhood who came to buy bread (at the bakery where we also lived) would say to her, "The foreclosure announcement came out." They rubbed salt in the wound because that meant my dad couldn't pay. When my mom asked the question, my dad replied, "God gives,

God takes away...", totally detached and stoic. It was a great lesson in detachment; perhaps deep down he felt like crap, as we say in good local slang, but the point is that it wasn't the response I expected. I have many other beautiful memories with my siblings, but another memory that engraved in my memory is something that happened to me in that cinema, and that has to do with my relationship with my mom not being better. I don't know why I focused on my mom. Let me tell you the story: a great-uncle from my mom's side who came to visit us from time to time, once came to the cinema and since the cinema was nearby, I accompanied him. You know how kids are, more sociable; I accompanied him to watch the movie. It was dark, and suddenly I felt he was touching me inappropriately! he was an older man, in his fifties, and I was about 5 or 6 years old. I'm going back and forth in the story, but we're talking about ugly things that impacted my life. That marked my existence a lot because even at five years old I knew that was wrong, but in my innocence, I didn't know what to do and I froze. I only remember that when the intermission came, because at that time they showed two movies for the same price, when the first movie ended and the intermission came it was when sodas, toast, Hot Dogs, etc. were for sale... I remember my mom was at the sales stand, because that was another way to help my dad and contribute to the household economy, and I remember seeing her from afar and saying to myself, "If my mom knew what this man just did to me".

And I thought, "She should have been looking out for me! and there she is... concerned with sales, trying to sell everything she can." At that moment, I internally blamed her for what had happened to me.

For almost 40 years, I didn't talk about it with anyone. Now I can talk about it because I'm in my 60s, and I've had many years of therapy, so it's less difficult for me. It's sad and ugly, and it's part of my story. So, I think that affected my relationship with men because I learned to always be defensive, to be afraid of getting hurt. I tell you, there's something innate in human beings, God put a "chip" in us that lets you know when something is right and when it's not. I was a victim at that moment, but I didn't know how to handle it, how could I? I was a child! Because at some point, I also thought it was my fault. In those days, in the sixties, the issue of child abuse was inconceivable, and no one told you it was wrong or how to protect yourself, but there's something instinctive in you that tells you it's not right.

The saddest thing about that terrible experience was the damage it did to my relationship with my mom because, this was something I eventually talked about with the psychologist as an adult, and I realized I was still punishing her for it. Many years later, I talked to her about it, she remained silent; I also told my dad and he remained silent, the guilty man had already died. Talking to my parents about it was part of the healing process.

So, Genesis, before moving on to the next stage of this story and revisiting the theme of abuse and infidelity in my parents' relationship, I just want to remind you that we all have the capacity to transform ourselves, as my parents did. Yes, they made many mistakes, and he especially is one of the "bad guys" in this story, but it was more than that because he went through a process of change, of improvement, thanks to my mom showing him that forgiveness is the best expression of love. She saw the rough diamond that came into her life, and through love and perseverance, they together managed to "polish" themselves. He transformed into a man of God because he came to know His word, to ask for forgiveness, and to reconcile with himself before departing. They lived together for 47 years, and he left this world surrounded by the love of all his children because, in his own way, he made each of us feel special.

Over the years, my mom made several attempts to leave the situation we were in, but ultimately gave up on her plans when she thought about raising us without a father figure. She even tried to travel "north" to start a new life on her own, aiming to send remittances and provide us with a better material life. However, when the time came to leave, she was moved by how small and defenseless we were. Now I am grateful that she did not do it, because our childhood would have been extremely difficult, and we would have experienced real feelings of abandonment, which are very hard to overcome.

My mom lived to be a mother and she did it exceptionally well. Eventually, she also had her moment of redemption: she knelt before my half-siblings and asked for forgiveness. Reconciliation requires humility, but ultimately it elevates you. All my half-siblings visited her during her illness and were present at her funeral. I see this outcome as another definition of success and redemption: achieving forgiveness from those you have hurt.

SIMONA

Another Lesson About Forgiveness

Simona was my maternal grandmother. Born in Mazatenango, in the west of Guatemala, at the age of 15 her brother-in-law threatened her with death if she did not elope with him. An atrocity. She was the daughter of peasant parents who worked and lived on a coffee farm whose owner was a European, fair-skinned, wealthy landowner. My grandfather, the life partner of Simona's sister, abducted her under threat of death; he was at least twenty years older than her. We affectionately called my grandmother "Moncha". The plan was to elope one night - which my grandmother accepted out of fear - and take the train from the town of Mazatenango to the city of Guatemala. In the early 1900s, Guatemala's conservative and macho culture strongly condemned a woman who had been 'touched' by a man outside of marriage. So, they left on the night train and the next morning, upon arriving at a town along the way, her parents and the police caught up with them, as she was underage, and they had fled without getting married.

My grandmother told me about the scare she had when she saw her parents bring the police, so they walked back all day to their village from where they had fled, a form of punishment. Upon arriving at the courthouse, the judge gave them the option to marry or spend a few months in jail, because they had committed an 'act against morality' by eloping. The one who answered the judge's question was her mother, my great-grandmother Isabel, imagine! And she said, "marriage". A 15-year-old woman had no voice or vote over her own destiny. Thus began a married life with someone she truly did not love. My grandfather was very harsh and demanding, he gave her eight children, I imagine many conceived under threat. She separated from him as soon as the youngest son reached adulthood. Over the years, I asked my grandmother how she could care for him in old age and forgive him for so many years of violence. Her response was very selfless and a great lesson for me, she managed to view her past with compassion and forgave him, because forgiveness is the only way to free the victim, it was the only way to live the rest of her life in peace. She died at the age of 95. One of the legacies I received from her was reinforcing in me the seed of faith in an Almighty God, independence in the golden years, and enjoying solitude. I hold on to that.

My great-grandmother could also have been abused, not by her partner, but by the farm owner, a very strong accusation, but very likely, since Moncha was the only daughter with fair skin and hazel color eyes among a group of children with Mayan features. My grandmother told me that she remembered seeing the farm owner enter the house and lock himself in with my great-grandmother, right under the nose of her husband, who couldn't say anything because they lived on the coffee plantation owner's land in exchange for hard work. Some kind of slavery in the late 1800s.

Chapter Two

The Seed of Success

At the age of 10 or 11, I began to realize that Guatemala felt small to me. Someone who impacted me greatly was a teacher I had in the final years of primary school, Miss Virginia (Vicky), whose last name I prefer not to mention. I remember well that she used to tell her female students: "A woman's passport is education," and she repeated it constantly. She also said: "You should not be the generation of women who are only meant to have children. Study! Study, girls! A woman was not born just to have children and stay at home. A woman can be many other things and not depend on a man. Have your own resources! Travel, but first, you must study very hard!" That impacted me greatly because from then on, I decided not to follow pre-established models and rebelled against anything that was following patterns imposed by society. On one hand, it was good, but on the other hand, it was bad because then I took on an arrogant attitude of "I'm not going to do things to please anyone else, I'm going to do what I want." Although I always had a rebellious spirit, I still do, ha, ha, ha!

Now I regret applying that concept so broadly because from that time on, I didn't want to do anything that I owed to anyone, I did not want anybody saying, "Oh! She's a doctor because her husband paid for her education!" or "She traveled because her husband took her!" or "She got promoted because she slept with someone!" So, I decided not to follow established patterns for myself, including having a traditional family. That was a big mistake, a huge arrogance. One thing I do thank my mom for is that she quickly realized that I liked to study, and she decided to support me even though she had very little education herself. She only went up to fifth grade, two years more than my dad, she didn't even finish primary school. She wasn't educated, but she was very wise.

From the fight I witnessed between my parents, I realized that the strongest one will always be the winner, and I decided to be strong. They say you should outgrow those models and shake off all those inheritances left by your parents, and there comes a point in life when you're no longer at the age to have superheroes, but for me, my dad was my superhero until he died. Sometimes I must remind myself that he was human too and that he also had flaws, made mistakes, was a sinner, but overall, I always admired him a lot for his strong and determined character. Despite his weaknesses, for me, the ones to blame were always the women who followed him, not him! It was their fault! Why did they follow him? Its not his fault for being handsome and daring, Ha, ha, ha! Why is it that when you love someone so much, you forgive them for everything?

If I remember correctly, he hadn't realized that I was getting good grades. One day, I went to the residence of the nuns of the Belgian School to talk to them, around seven in the evening, accompanied by a friend we'll call "la China." We were about 14 or 15 years old at the time. The nuns lived on Guadalupe Street, in Zone 10 in Guatemala City. We introduced ourselves and explained our economic situation. The nuns gave us a scholarship, and that's why I went to the Belgian School, one of the best in the country, because I had good grades and the nuns decided to give us an opportunity.

On the other hand, I remember that Miss Vicky, who I already mentioned, influenced my life a lot, she always used to say: "Let's see, Villarreal, the gifted one, go and ask your classmates for today's homework." You can't imagine how much that comment filled me. That teacher made me believe in myself! Gifted, I don't know, but I did like to read and study. I learned about Christopher Columbus's voyages sitting on the toilet, ha, ha, ha! It was "Toilette Reading," as they call it now, ha, ha, ha! I think it was my persistence combined with the encouragement and motivation she, as a teacher, gave me that pushed me to try to be better every day. When someone believes in you, they give you wings!

Génesis:

Thanks for sharing, Mom. Now, tell me, what dreams did you have?

Mónica:

I think one's dreams depend on age. At six, I wanted to be an opera singer, but in a third-world country in the 60s and 70s, our music classes consisted of watching the teacher play the piano, singing the national anthem, and learning the flag prayer. If you were lucky, they talked a little about Beethoven. That was all. The chances of being able to attend music classes or go to the national conservatory as a student in a public school, with 14 siblings, forget it! So, what were the chances of learning music? You don't realize it, but you start forgetting your dreams because your reality is different.

At ten, I wanted to be a flight attendant because they were all tall and beautiful, spoke another language, and I already wanted to travel a lot. Then I wanted to be a Certified

Translator or interpreter when I was 15 or 17, and that's why I came to the United States because I wanted to be an interpreter. I got into Georgetown University, I even enrolled in translation classes, I studied for a year. I regretted not passing the certification exams and got frustrated. Maybe that's a dream to fulfill later. This goal transformed into the desire to stay and gain my independence through a good job where I could grow.

Génesis:

Tell me about your first love, who was it?

Mónica:

My first crush was my neighbor, the brother of a very dear friend. Many years later, I found out that my friend, his sister, told him that I liked him, and he replied, "I can't be with a girl like Mónica," because he knew about the drug problem he had. He died young. There are many conspiracy theories about his death. After that teenage crush, I became friends with who later became my first husband, that's another topic that left me many lessons, such as learning to let go of someone who doesn't love you. Going into details would take days to recount. The next significant love was my second husband, a grumpy foreigner who had adaptation problems when he arrived in Guatemala because this episode of my life was when I returned to Guatemala after many years. From this relationship, I learned that the most important thing in life is your physical and mental health and that the "self" within you, who you are, is not negotiable.

From childhood, one of my mom's advices was that a woman has to endure everything from a man, that a woman doesn't speak ill of her partner. No matter how the man is, you should never speak ill of him, and for that reason, she taught us to respect and not judge my dad, to always thank him for everything he gave us, and those teachings strengthened the love between father and children, so we always accepted him no matter what. In adolescence, Guatemalan mothers, grandmothers, and aunts used to say that a woman falls in love and gets married only once in life, and she must marry as a virgin. For many years, I put off having a boyfriend because I thought I had to marry only once in life and that was too much pressure for me, it terrified me. Over time, I learned that you could fall in love more than once.

In the meantime, between my marriages, I felt butterflies in my stomach several times, and I remember one especially, a former colleague from the 90s whom for years I lost track of and now I know he's on the other side of the world, married, with children, and to whom I wish all the best. I would like to feel those butterflies in my stomach again.

My Hero, date unknown

The author with three of her siblings in 1965

CHAPTER THREE

Taking Risks and Overcoming Obstacles

Here begins the adventure of leaving Guatemala and emigrating north. Since I was a child, Guatemala seemed small to me. I didn't want to be one of those young mothers who came to ask for credit at my parents' bakery, with a belly, a child clinging to their dress on each side, in flip-flops, asking for two quetzals (Guatemala's currency) of bread on credit because they didn't have anything to eat that day. From an early age, I knew that wasn't what I wanted for myself.

At the age of 20, material goals included having a car, a house, and lots of purses (ha, ha, ha!) and financially supporting my family. Immaterial goals mainly included higher education, meeting interesting and intelligent people, exploring other countries, and, above all, earning the respect of my colleagues, whom I considered intelligent and inspiring individuals. Initially, upon arriving in the United States, I only wanted to obtain a good education to return to Guatemala and secure a good job in a solid company. Many immigrants come to the United States with the idea of "trying their luck": "I'll just save up 5 thousand dollars and go back to start a business," I would tell myself... Ha, ha, ha! That's what many of us say, driven by the nostalgia of returning to our homeland.

Génesis:

Tell us, how do you come to the determination to emigrate? I understand what you didn't want, but tell us how you arrive at that decision to leave that scenario and choose to emigrate to Washington, D.C.?

Mónica:

Well, ever since I was in the Belgian nuns' school, I realized that girls traveled a lot because they could, but I didn't have the resources. Many of my classmates came to the United States or Europe on exchanges. Additionally, in our Guatemalan culture, it was already known that studying outside of Guatemala gave you more prestige; it was assumed that education was better than in our Latin American countries, and I wanted that too. Also, the fact that my dad traveled to the U.S.A. every year and brought us gifts, as well as speaking wonders of the United States, influenced me; I also wanted to see those wonders. I began to feel that Guatemala did not offer enough opportunities. Besides, I wanted to free myself from my father's yoke, which was so strict. I saw what happened to my sister Anita, who had almost been forced into marriage because my dad had found her kissing her boyfriend, not even doing anything else, just kissing, and he confined her. I saw that he didn't let her graduate from high school, and having an education was my great dream. One piece of advice my mom gave me was: "Your dad has many children, don't expect him to leave you anything, not because his effort isn't worth it, but because whatever you want in your life, a house, a car, travels, etc., you have to seek it, you have to work for it because nobody owes you anything."

Génesis:

And with your dad being so strict, how did he allow you to come to the United States?

Mónica:

Ah! That was another adventure. It turns out that he went to the American Consulate to apply for visas for my mom and me. At that time, more than one person could enter to the interview with the US Consul, so he took our passports. He said we would accompany him on one of his many trips to the United States; he had been traveling 'up north' since 1956, so the consulate already had his record, and they gave us the visa immediately. But shortly after, my dad had legal problems. He fired an employee from his carpentry shop for theft, and the employee sued him for wrongful dismissal, which left him grounded and unable to leave the country. With the tickets bought, I said to him: "Dad, forgive me, but I'm going". My mom decided to accompany me. So, we traveled together, she and I, we arrived in New Orleans and took a Greyhound bus to

Washington D.C., where a cousin offered us her apartment to stay. I will be eternally grateful to her for that gesture.

We stayed in my cousin's apartment for a couple of months. I had $2000, all my savings, and I thought we could live on that for a whole year, Ha, ha, ha! What a fool I was! A lady who lived there took me to work cleaning offices. It was hard for me to accept that I had come to the United States to do that job, but I promised myself it would only be a steppingstone to something more. Although many times I felt bad, I also convinced myself that there was no undignified work. Soon I started working at a Howard Johnson hotel, cleaning rooms, and again I felt like the crown I was wearing as "Miss Guatemala" was falling off. My mom had already started working as a nanny. One day, cleaning the bathtub in a hotel room, I had this conversation: "My God, I don't know what you want from me, but I'm sure this is temporary, I'm sure you will help me, I'm sure you will take me to something better; this will be my steppingstone".

Shortly after, I decided to send job applications to different organizations. In one of these organizations, a knowledge bank that we'll call "the Bank," they replied that they received 10,000 applications a year and that they would "In due Time" consider mine. I wasn't going to wait for 10,000 applications to pass before mine. With clothes unsuitable for June's heat, with a temperature of 90°F, covering myself up to my neck due to an allergy that looked like hickeys, ha, ha, ha! I went out to knock on doors. I knew that a former vice president of Guatemala worked at the bank, and I showed up at one of the lobbies, trying to get the receptionist to let me in, but without success. I had no experience in making appointments with professionals in these organizations. How naive. I said, "I want to speak with Mr. Alleman," and she replied that without a prior appointment, they couldn't let me in. However, I noticed that across the street there was another lobby of the same bank. I had already learned my lesson.

I lied to the second receptionist: "Tell Mr. Alleman that I bring a message from his sister-in-law and that I need to speak with him, please give me 10 minutes. My name is Mónica Villarreal." Desperate measures in desperate times. Yes, I had been a student of his sister-in-law. He was wonderful with me. I will always be grateful because the first thing I told him was: "I'm from Guatemala, my name is Mónica Villarreal. Yes, I was a student of your sister-in-law, but I lied because otherwise they wouldn't let me in. I'm not bringing you any message; all I ask is that you help me get the pre-employment exams. I just want to have that step forward."

He was so kind to me! He asked if I had anything to eat and if I had winter clothes. He gave me several names of contacts in different international organizations. Of all the names he gave me, he was the only one who really helped me, because the other doors I knocked on didn't receive me, even if they were compatriots. The next day, he called my cousin's apartment himself and said to me, "You have an interview tomorrow at 9 a.m." He acted immediately. My dad didn't appreciate him as a politician because he had strong opinions about politics, but there I told him: "Dad, forget it. Mr. Alleman may be very socialist, but he opened doors for me and helped me a lot. He just missed giving me money." I will always be very grateful to him, and hopefully God took that into account when he arrived in heaven. That's where the ladder started, that ladder that took me many years to climb from one step to another. I started as a typist. Of course, the day they hired me was wow! What excitement! They asked me if I wanted to cover for someone's vacation and supposedly, I went to the interview, and right away I stayed! I hit the jackpot!

To secure that job, one of the challenges I faced was that, after so many exams, interviews, psychological tests, and the famous analogies, I failed the typing test, which was an essential requirement for employment, not even as a filing clerk! If I didn't type a certain number of words per minute on an IBM typewriter since personal computers didn't exist at that time. Anyone reading this and thinking about the nonexistence of computers would be surprised, like my nephew who asks me, "How did you survive without computers?" Ha, ha, ha! So, what happened was that I was so nervous that I made many mistakes. I wanted to fight for myself; I felt bad! My own nerves betrayed me. Mrs. Marieta González, in charge of these exams, said to me:

-"You were very nervous; you're allowed a maximum of five mistakes, you had seven. Go home and practice, and I'll give you another chance next Monday." Just eight days later.

She didn't know that I didn't have a typewriter at home, as my cousin lived very modestly. Fortunately, across the street from my cousin's apartment was an Episcopal church with a Chilean pastor. Pastor Iván, I don't remember his last name, helped me even though I told him I was Catholic. I said, "Look, I have to take an exam." He let me practice on the typewriter in his office every day. He was another angel that God put in my path.

So, the next Monday, I took the exam, and I was calmer. God bless those who give second chances, because we all need them. What I want to say is that I learned during that transition from cleaning offices to working at the bank, that not only Americans but also within the Latino community, we label ourselves and believe that cleaning and childcare are the only things we can do, just like my cousin's tenant did, she saw me as Latina and offered to take me to do cleaning, without a second thought, it was her way of helping me and she didn't imagine that I could do something more than that, a sad assumption. I accepted to go because the budget was tight and because I knew I would learn something useful.

One of the things that I would like to emphasize is to invite our Latin culture not to judge those in the same culture, limiting ourselves to other opportunities, just because we are immigrants from Latin America and Central America. Coming from a poor country, being a woman, and having a mestizo appearance does not mean that you have no education or that you are dumb, and that you can only perform cleaning and childcare jobs.

The motivation I had to stay in the United States and "ride my macho" (a popular expression in Guatemala synonymous with firmness) was to tell myself, "I'm not leaving the U.S.A. without a college degree." In my house, with so many children, the idea of going to college was just a distant dream, something that wasn't even talked about because it seemed impossible. In those days in the 80s, in a politically unstable country like Guatemala, going to college was risking being labeled a communist and risk disappearing. Also, the opportunities to get a good job were scarce.

The main reason I had to leave Guatemala was to study, and the second motivation was to help my family. I knew that to help my family, I first had to be well myself. Those of us who have emigrated have paid a very high price for pursuing those dreams and desires to support the family, although over time, the beneficiaries either do not know it, have forgotten it, or simply do not care who sacrificed so that they could have the security they live in. I'm sure many immigrants identify themselves with me in this aspect. The price I refer to is the pain of leaving family and friends behind, missing out on important events such as Christmas parties, weddings, baptisms, and birthdays, which are always excuses to gather and strengthen the family bond that we still miss after 40 years. Still, I recognize that the best gift my parents gave me was, on the one hand, the gift of my mother's support, who always said to my father:

"Let her study, don't make negative comments." On the other hand, my father's love, and respect.

In my generation, the role of women was defined by getting married and having children. The symbol of success was a lasting marriage, even if your husband mistreated you, having many children, and being a successful mother in the sense of ensuring that your children were well cared for, fed, and in good schools. My mom always believed in me, despite objections from my dad, who used to say, "Why do you study so much? You'll drive yourself crazy!" He would lean in close and say, "Men don't like women who think... Women who think don't get married. I don't want you to become an old maid, marry a poor man, just get married!" Ha, ha, ha! My mom always contradicted him: "Let her study, it's good for her to excel." Today they would call him misogynistic, and thankfully, I didn't listen to him, ha, ha, ha!

My mom kept the balance, and that was another great gift. My dad was strict, though not a tyrant; he had a soft spot, was kind, protective, and a good provider. The greatest gift he gave me was the freedom to spread my wings when he came to Washington, D.C. to travel back to Guatemala with my mom in December 1984 (remember we she and I had emigrated together). He missed her a lot and told her they would return to Guatemala. At that moment, he sought a way to evade the legal restrictions. He left through the border with El Salvador, by land, as there were not so many controls in those remote areas. Once in El Salvador, he bought a ticket and came to Washington D.C., playing a prank on the Guatemalan government! They returned by bus because there were not so many controls again.

As they prepared to return to Guatemala, my father asked me, "Are you certain you don't wish to come back with us? There's still time for you to join us. What will you do here all alone, without any family?" I replied, "No, I'm staying here. I want to attend the university." He responded, "I'll pay for your university, but in Guatemala, as finances are tight here." He never made this offer to any of my siblings. I felt special, because I understood that his financial means were limited.

So, I told him, "Daddy, I want to study here, and I want to pay for it myself." We both choked up. He simply said, "Well, if that's what you want, so be it," and he sighed. He gave me his blessing and said, "The day you get tired of this, the day you grow weary of this, you can hop on the first plane and head back to Guatemala. Your home awaits you there, your Tata awaits you there." His words still move me deeply. From that moment on, I knew I had a sanctuary in Guatemala.

Over the years, I've come to understand how challenging it must have been for my father to let his child go, and the greatest gift he gave me was respecting my decision. He granted me the freedom to spread my wings, to forge my own path, to pursue my dreams. That's why the happiest day of my life was the day I graduated from university, knowing it was the fruit of my own labor. Though the occasion was clouded by the tragic plane crash that claimed my brother José's life, a topic I'd rather not dwell on now due to its painful nature.

When I arrived at the Bank, the struggle I faced was for professional respect. I quickly identified the barriers. The first was that my English wasn't as fluent. The certification of Bilingual Secretariat (high school) was the furthest I had gone, and there weren't many hopes of accessing university education soon, as we know, the cost in the United States was, and still is, extremely high. Therefore, obtaining a college degree on my own would take longer than it would for any average American. I never felt poor, though, I want to make that clear, because my dad made sure to boost my ego. As I mentioned before, my dad treated me like a queen. Later, when he was dying, I realized I wasn't the only queen; he had eight daughters, and he said the same to all of us! Ha, ha, ha!

It took me many years, but I managed to be the first of 15 children to have a college degree. So, another barrier to achieving my goal was the financial aspect.

God provided me with help by sending understanding bosses who supported me, allowing me, sometimes, to leave work 10 minutes early or reviewing my university documents. One of those people, to whom I owe a lot, is Tammy, one of my supervisors, who on the day I finished my bachelor's degree told me: "Now the master's, and then the doctorate." Tammy was another angel for me.

Another barrier, already in the workplace, was realizing that you are judged by your appearance. Having a Mayan-descendant build didn't help me in a world so politicized where the game is with more powerful countries than Central America. I felt discriminated against on several occasions. Some sociologists recognized at that time that white men had more opportunities to advance in the career ladder, and that a Central American woman with indigenous or mestizo appearance was not so fortunate.

I remember a supervisor at work, from an important area in the organization, who at one point said to me:

-"Ah, Central American, huh! Central American women are very submissive, you need to change" -with her accent from South America-. That's when the protective bubble my dad had put me in as a child started to burst, because her comment made me feel bad, diminished. That's when I began to realize that you are indeed judged by appearance. However, at the same time, I owe her something good... she gave me a business card of a makeup artist from Neiman Marcus.

-"Have her teach you how to do your makeup" -she said-. I spent over $200 on Chanel makeup the day I went; that was a lot of money back in 1985. Although I initially feared this supervisor, as she had made many assistants cry with her despotism, over the years, I learned a lot from her and ended up admiring her. She was a real diva, a professional executive, impeccable, and I decided to take the good from her examples.

Returning to the notion of "how you're perceived is how you're treated," without a university degree and with a submissive personality (believe it or not, at some point I was submissive and insecure), aware of my limitations and lacking connections, I didn't know how to socialize. I detested the cocktails and social events at my job because they meant a lot of exposure for me, and besides, I'm introverted. I realized I would have to be a bit more assertive, confident, and friendly, so I challenged myself to attend every social event until I overcame that shyness.

Back then, the word "assertive" didn't exist to make sure my opinions were considered and heard.

I've mentioned how often I felt displaced or ignored. That's where I understood I had to prepare more, work harder, and be more assertive, more confident, and not "shrink," as we say in Guatemala, when my opinions weren't heard. So, I learned and changed, and I had to persist in achieving my goals. Many times, I felt like my ideas weren't listened to, but they were when expressed by someone else, especially a man. In other words, it took me years to earn that professional respect. For this, I became more aggressive, more demanding of myself and others, more assertive. Perhaps I lacked a bit of balance because in such a politicized world, being too intense isn't good either. By the late 90s, thankfully, the world was changing, the role of women was becoming more relevant, and I had more education, so they began to take me into account a little more. I had climbed a few steps on the ladder.

It took me many years to shed the title of secretary and assistant to be recognized as a professional. It also took me years to finish my university degree, as I was working full-time and studying at night. I often slept only four hours because between finishing classes at College Park at 10 p.m., getting home to do homework or finish some office work, it was already 3 a.m. In this process of analysis and reflection, one of the gifts I have received has been to share this story and realize that I wasn't perfect. Perhaps I didn't reach higher, but I did the best I could with the tools I had at that time. It's not so much what others demand of us, but what we demand of ourselves, and thus we enjoy life less. Take note, my dear Génesis, don't be so critical of yourself.

Another thing I learned was not to take anything personally. This too was the result of conversations with other colleagues who were brave enough to tell me, "You're taking this personally." It serves us well to be less sensitive and not think that everything we're told is meant to hurt us. Some people might indeed want to make us feel bad, but that is the moment when you must decide to turn what you're hearing around and say, no! They're telling me this so that I can improve. This shift in thinking requires humility, something I didn't always have and something I continue to work on.

Génesis:

Give us a concrete list of the most important advices you would give to a younger person to achieve their goals and find purpose in life:

Mónica:

If I could convey something to the new generations about achieving goals, what is fundamental to finding meaning in life, it would be the following:

On a personal and practical level:

• Define what success means to you and what your goals are, both material and immaterial.

• Focus on those goals and don't let anything distract you. Persist in reaching them, no matter how long it takes. It took me years to complete my first master's degree, but I did it!

- Strive to surpass yourself. To ensure that others are well, you must first be well yourself. Remember that you need to put on the oxygen mask before helping others.

- Develop a life plan and save for your old age. In Latin America, and specifically in Guatemala, we don't have the habit of saving or planning for old age. When you receive your salary, pay yourself first, meaning set aside 10 percent to save and for emergencies. If you can't save 10 percent, no matter how much, but save! Make a monthly budget and stick to it religiously. Keep track of even the smallest expense, as everything adds up. This includes paying off debts and contributing to your community or church. It is also important to take care of our elderly relatives, especially our parents. I was taught that children should take care of their parents in their old age. It is part of being generous to those who have less than you, and in my experience, the Universe returns what you give, multiplied many times. However, help of love and generosity, not out of self-interest or because you think the person deserves it.

• Seek reconciliation with those you know you need to. Ask for or give forgiveness. This will free you from the burden that prevents you from growing. Anger and resentment are poisons that spread to others. For this, you will need to dedicate time in silence to listen to your God of Light, Universe, Higher Consciousness, or whatever you call it.

In the professional realm, I would say:

• Don't take everything personally. Let go of what bothers you and move forward objectively. If you find it difficult, take a coffee break and clear your mind; you'll have a fresh perspective on the issue.

• Be assertive and work on overcoming shyness. Practice will make you an expert.

• Seek out a mentor, whether in your workplace or community. They should be someone you admire and want to emulate.

• Persist in being a contributing member in meetings.

• Cultivate humility and control your ego. Evaluate whether your reactions are motivated by pride, arrogance, or envy.

Especially to my fellow countrymen, I would say: "Let's stop being so sensitive and let's be more assertive. Speak up more often!" If someone says something you don't like in a meeting, don't withdraw, or get angry; stay at the table. All of this is also part of loving yourself.

Mónica:

Apologies, I digressed a bit... let's get back on track.

One lesson I learned, expanding on the topic of ego management, was during one of the selection processes in which I participated many times. During an interview, a candidate asked the head of the panel (potential boss):

"What is the secret to having a successful career in this organization?"

The interviewer's response was:

"Knowing how to handle egos." A great truth. Those of us who stayed working for 20 or 30 years in the same organization achieved it thanks to learning, in one way or another, how to manage those egos, including our own. Although newer generations don't stay in the same job that long, the principle remains valid.

Personally, I am very satisfied with my accomplishments. I had a fulfilling career, which could have reached greater heights, yes, but it was a satisfying career, nonetheless. I lacked assertiveness and better ego management; if I had known how to handle it, I would have gone further, been more successful, and had a greater impact. However, lamenting doesn't serve much purpose, and I must learn to be more generous with myself. One should be more compassionate with oneself, revisit our own story, and be kinder to that story.

Génesis:

In conclusion, professionally speaking, what is the greatest gift you can leave to a future generation?

Mónica:

I would tell them, "Stay at the table, seated or standing, but stay" and these are the words of a female manager from my former job, a very, very successful one.

When things don't go as expected, or you feel belittled for being a woman or young and inexperienced, stay at the table! Don't leave, keep participating! Keep giving your best! This attitude is part of perseverance and, in the end, it's a Christian principle.

If you fall, get up! and continue your path. Be humble in acknowledging that the first ego you must manage is your own, because while getting a job at a big organization is a great achievement, staying there and building a successful career is another. There is always room to aspire for more. Although this generation already knows it and is proving it. Organizational loyalty has disappeared, and younger people are thinking more about themselves, which is good if there's a balance and they also think about others.

PART THREE

"When we are no longer able to change a situation, we are challenged to change ourselves."

Viktor Frankl

CHAPTER FOUR

The Transition

In this story, transition refers to the shift from a busy working life to retirement, from one country to another, from one marital status to another, and from seeking new goals. The challenge of retirement has been to slow down the train that was racing at full speed in a busy professional career and find a new incentive through an active and peaceful life, learning to create my own agenda every day.

Learning to enjoy the gift of free time and embrace whatever life presents.

So, it's time to work on myself, on my peace of mind, and that's why I decided to give myself a chance at a second marriage, which as you know, didn't work out.

Yesterday I said the forbidden word in my house, which was: "I'm bored," because my mom used to say: "Are you bored? - Let's see, dear... there's the broom!" There's always something to do at home, we learned never to say the word "bored" in my house, ha, ha, ha! So, I've now reached this stage in my life, these last few months, where I tell myself: "I'm not bored," ha, ha, ha! However, I've also learned that boredom has its upside, because that's when you start looking for something to entertain yourself with, and in a creative way.

CHAPTER FIVE

Finding a New Meaning in Life

Now that I've reached retirement, achieved my goals, obtained the education I wanted, helped my family, tried to start a family which didn't work out, traveled as much as I wanted, and in my personal definition, achieved the success I sought, I asked myself: What now? What is the purpose of getting up every morning?

I asked myself: Who am I? Where am I? Where am I going?

Genesis:

Do you think that returning from Guatemala to the D.C. area is because of that same reason? Because you're seeking time for yourself and a new meaning in your life?

Mónica:

-Yes. It's part of the search for the meaning of my life. Because if not now, when? It's now that I'm in my sixties, if I don't seek my own happiness, my own purpose, who will do it for me? We all spend our lives searching for happiness and peace, we have many distractions when we are younger, so now is the time to redefine success through new goals, and that's a new purpose. We all dream of doing many things when we retire, but we don't know. I thought I was going to teach at a university because I have excellent work experience. Although I found myself faced with technology that I struggle to understand, there is a certain personal experience that cannot be found on the internet. I must confess that today's new generation, the one I thought I was going to teach is teaching me instead, ha, ha, ha!... And that now younger people can find everything on Google, so I was a bit intimidated, I must admit, and I contradict myself thinking that old concepts of knowledge are still relevant, and I hope to contribute in that way in the future. Another goal to fulfill, another motivation that gives meaning to my life.

Génesis:

What do you mean by "if not now, when?"

Mónica:

It means that it's time to revisit all those dreams I had before and that, for one reason or another, I discarded or postponed. It's time to pick them up again and analyze why I abandoned or postponed them and determine if I still find them interesting. Some of those dreams may have lost relevance over time. This review also involves being flexible when evaluating my personal values and the influences inherited from previous generations. Not everything we have inherited is beneficial, so it's crucial to do a mental cleanup of what no longer serves us, even if it involves traditions that bind us to our family of origin.

Transgenerational Inheritances

There are transgenerational inheritances that become a heavy burden, such as the idea that you only marry once in life. I learned that this is not necessarily true, with all due respect to my mother and female ancestors. Nor should we tolerate any kind of behavior from our partner; our physical and mental health are priorities. Coming from a line of abused women does not mean that we are doomed to repeat that history. Being humble does not equate to being foolish, but rather to being wise; this I learned after analyzing my mother's life. Sometimes it's okay to stay silent during an argument; we must learn to accept defeat and acknowledge that we cannot always win; all of this speaks to ego management and emotional intelligence. There are also positive inheritances that parents leave us. In my case, from my father, I learned to take pride in the work I do and to put my personal touch on it, to do it well from the start. I learned the first lessons about the God of love who does not judge that we are all unique, to have self-esteem, to respect my fellow beings.

From my mother, I learned not only household chores, although not all stayed with me, but also learned about generosity towards those who have less. She gave me the first lessons in empathy, to always be productive, to be independent, and in short, the words that best describe her come from Proverbs 31:

"The Woman of Valor"

"Who can find a virtuous woman? For her price is far above rubies. The heart of her husband doth safely trust in her, so that he shall have no need of spoil. She will do him good and not evil all the days of her life. She seeketh wool, and flax, and worketh willingly with her hands. She is like the merchants' ships; she bringeth her food from afar. She riseth also while it is yet night, and giveth meat to her household, and a portion to her maidens. She considereth a field, and

buyeth it: with the fruit of her hands she planteth a vineyard. She girdeth her loins with strength, and strengtheneth her arms. She perceiveth that her merchandise is good: her candle goeth not out by night. She layeth her hands to the spindle, and her hands hold the distaff. She stretcheth out her hand to the poor; yea, she reacheth forth her hands to the needy. She is not afraid of the snow for her household: for all her household are clothed with scarlet. She maketh herself coverings of tapestry; her clothing is silk and purple. Her husband is known in the gates when he sitteth among the elders of the land. She maketh fine linen, and selleth it; and delivereth girdles unto the merchant. Strength and honour are her clothing; and she shall rejoice in time to come. She openeth her mouth with wisdom; and in her tongue is the law of kindness. She looketh well to the ways of her household, and eateth not the bread of idleness. Her children arise up, and call her blessed; her husband also, and he praiseth her.

Many daughters have done virtuously, but thou excellest them all. Favour is deceitful, and beauty is vain: but a woman that feareth the Lord, she shall be praised."

This is precisely what she was: hardworking, entrepreneurial, protective of her family, and deeply religious. I remember seeing her sewing dresses for her clients until midnight or later, always singing or humming to the rhythm of the marimba, and getting up at dawn, even before the sun had risen, to attend to the bakery. She evangelized and rescued a few young women from prostitution, always opened the doors of her home to those in need, worked shoulder to shoulder with my father, and was content with very little material attachment.

In the twilight of their lives and during the terminal stage of my father's illness, I received one of the greatest lessons on true forgiveness from my mother. I had traveled from Washington, D.C. to Guatemala to be with him in his final days, one of the most difficult journeys of my life. One day, I descended from the second floor to the first floor where my parents' bedroom was, to reach the kitchen where my mother was. I had to pass through the hallway in front of their bedroom.

As I passed through the open door of the bedroom, I saw my father unconscious and a woman sitting in a chair next to his bed. I had never seen her before, but my female instinct told me it was her, Marion-eta, the former mistress of my father with whom he had had the last three children. I was furious! I asked my mother, who was in the kitchen:

"Is the lady sitting there Marion-eta? What is she doing here? Don't you see she reminds him of his sins? I will tell her to leave, she has no business being here!"

My mother replied:

"Stop! I gave her permission to come and say goodbye to him! She asked me, and I granted it. Besides, there's nothing left to fight about, because in the end, he stayed with me, he never abandoned me, and he's dying in my house."

I was speechless because she stood her ground and didn't allow me to kick her out of my house. Not only had she forgiven my father for his infidelity, but she was also forgiving her! I was used to fights over a man's love in the style of a Latin soap opera, where women end up tangled in each other's hair, but my mother was different. She handled the situation with great dignity and granted that woman the same. Despite my complaints, my mother behaved like a true lady.

These legacies are part of who I am today; I choose the ones that I deem good and move forward.

Now, forgive me if I digressed again, and let's get back to the topic of finding a new sense of purpose in life... One of my failed dreams was to have a marriage and a family, although it was a late dream, it was one of the biggest disappointments, a disillusionment. Another disappointment occurred when I returned to Guatemala. Although I enjoyed my time there and am grateful for having had a comfortable life, I returned to Guatemala with a partner and a marriage that fell apart. I came back with the hope of having a stronger and lasting family connection, but after 15 days, a month, everyone returned to their routines, as is natural, and I understand that.

I have a big house that I bought with the hope of an adoption that never happened. Then, I thought I would live there with my husband and my sister. However, I separated from my husband, and I found that living with my sister didn't work. Two queens in one house, each feeling like the lady of the house... it simply didn't work. We love each other very much, but it's better for each of us to have our own space, and first, I had to accept uncertainty and the idea of an empty refuge. I ended up living alone in a big house, in the country that was always my refuge when things went wrong. Guatemala wasn't the paradise I expected. My sanctuary or refuge had faded away.

Génesis (after a moment of silence):

So, what is your definition of 'refuge' now, and how or where do you rebuild it?

Mónica:

My refuge was the place to escape from difficult situations, where I felt loved and loved, where I recharged my batteries. It was the place where I found peace, felt secure, and where joy returned to me in moments of sadness. Where is that now? I'll tell you later.

What I want to convey is that, although returning to Guatemala after so many years seemed like paradise, I discovered that there are things that bother me, like traffic, insecurity, and disorder.

What I love about Guatemala is the family unity, the more abundant economy, and the more active social life thanks to having an extended family. That makes you feel part of something. I adore the family unity in our culture; everything is a celebration, a party. It's very beneficial for mental health to see that, despite the difficulties, people are happy. In Washington D.C., I have many friends, although not much family. In the end, in both places, I spend a lot of time alone; perhaps it's a reality I must accept. It could be part of aging or simply a reflection of how society is today, as it seems to be a loneliness crisis in the world. Part of the process of finding peace and giving new meaning to my life is accepting that and seeking new challenges, building new refuges, like writing this story, reviewing my dreams, seeking to know my Creator better, and seeing what dreams I have left to fulfill, or simply creating new dreams.

The fact that I could fall in love again and feeling the excitement of being part of a family shows that there are still possibilities for me, that this stage of life isn't necessarily winter of my live. I want to believe that another spring is coming. It's a struggle that many retirees probably face feeling like life doesn't end when you retire, and it's something to fight for every day. The structure that used to be provided by a job; I now have to create for myself every day.

It also seems like life had value only because I belonged to something, to the circle of work, to an international organization that gave me a certain prestige. So, did life end when I left that job? No! The thing is, some of us become too attached to work, to an institution, and what that institution represented in our lives. That job was what took care of us and gave us a sense of belonging, it was our family. Retirement doesn't have to mean that winter has come to my life. In the cycle of life, winters, springs, autumns, and summers always come back.

Génesis:

Upon leaving that job, how do you work towards finding the path to peace?

Mónica:

By engaging in deep reflection and prayer. I am grateful for having time for myself, for my spirituality. So, from the moment I returned from Guatemala to the United States, without a partner, I went through a period of depression, inner emptiness, and apathy because I never imagined returning to Washington, D.C. alone. For me, the United States meant coming to work hard to study and help my family, and it turns out that those goals have already been achieved, and this plan to return alone was never part of the picture. So, how do I adjust to a plan that life has handed me? I must learn what to do with these lemons that fell on me. I decided to think of it as embarking on an adventure again, with the major difference being that at 20, I had fixed goals, and at 60, I am searching for new ones because I have already achieved all my previous goals. In this process of analysis, I realized that I was facing the need for a mental shift regarding my personal definition of important topics and concepts that had given me the adrenaline to move forward in previous years. Giving new meaning to familiar concepts and becoming more flexible, such as seeing boredom as an opportunity to be creative;

viewing fear of risk as prudence before acting because previously, I would dive in without considering the consequences; allowing myself to rest and seeing it as an opportunity to meditate; giving myself a second chance; learning that the toughest arguments can easily end with a 'you're right,' and that it's no longer worth trying to always be right because I have nothing to prove to anyone anymore.

I realized that it will probably be a period of trying out different projects until I find my way, the true purpose that God has for me. In this process, I noticed that I was so exhausted from romantic relationships that didn't solidify; some due to being prudish, others due to being demanding, some due to unrealistic expectations, and others due to boredom. In any case, I invested a lot in them, invested time, invested money. So, I got tired of giving, and I realized that it would now be better to dedicate that time and/or resources I used to give to boyfriends to my Creator. I acknowledged the lack of having a connection and a certain intimacy with someone, and I'm not talking in a carnal sense, but an emotional intimacy, and I decided that this intimacy would now be with God, with Jesus. I began asking God a lot to show me the way forward and asked where He wanted me.

I asked myself:

-Do I think about marriage or another romantic relationship again? Although I felt very empty to focus on a partner because one gets tired of giving and there comes a time when you need to receive, and that's the moment to stop and observe what things will fill your "love well" again. In my case, it's family unity, spending time with my friends, the unconditional love of my pets, my hobbies, prayer, and meditation. Part of the peace process has been accepting myself as I am: an immigrant, a Central American woman, with a few degrees, retired, I don't have goals, but I'm looking for them, and above all, I am a child of God.

Yes, I must admit that I have certain issues with commitment, a topic we will revisit later.

CHAPTER SIX

Embracing Uncertainty

To move beyond the stage of emptiness and apathy, I went through a period of uncertainty that halted me. I noticed that often, we cling to security and predictability, but what happens when life presents us with unexpected challenges? How can we find meaning amidst emptiness or chaos? I learned that there are specific steps to embrace uncertainty, and I'd like to share them here:

The Paradox of Uncertainty: Despite our efforts to avoid it, uncertainty is an inevitable part of life. Instead of resisting it, learning to embrace it allows us to grow and adapt. This requires patience with oneself.

Transformation Through Adversity: Through inspiring stories of individuals, like my mother and grandmother, who found new meaning despite facing unexpected or inexplicable challenges, we explore how adversity can be an opportunity for personal growth. These experiences teach us that even in the darkest moments, there is light and hope.

The Importance of Purpose: Through practical exercises and deep reflections, humans can **identify core values** and how we can align with them, even in times of darkness or emptiness. Here, meditation, prayer, or self-connection would be good examples.

Gratitude as a Guide: The daily practice of gratitude can transform our perspective and help us find beauty even in the most difficult moments. Through concrete examples such as walking your dog or taking a bike ride, you can learn to cultivate that attitude of gratitude that guides you towards a new sense of purpose and meaning. Make your effort and leave the outcome in the hands of your God of Light.

The Value of Silence: In this bustling, fast-paced modern world, the value of silence can be like an oasis of serenity and reflection. Amidst the constant noise of technology and the demands of everyday life, silence can be our refuge where we find inner peace and mental clarity. It is in those moments of calm where our minds can rest, free from the stress and anxiety that often overwhelm us. In silence, we can hear our own inner voice, connect with our deepest emotions, and better understand our needs and desires.

Silence serves as a reminder that true wisdom often resides precisely in tranquility. In this frantic world, learning to appreciate and cultivate the value of silence becomes an invaluable skill for finding balance and emotional well-being. It behooves us to nurture our personal spaces of silence so that we can listen to our inner voice, the voice of your God if you choose to call it that and savor that personal connection with our inner selves.

The Path Forward: I conclude this section with a gaze towards the future, reminding you that although uncertainty can be daunting, it's also an opportunity for reinvention and discovering new meaning in life.

Expanding on this theme of the path forward, I want to emphasize that embracing uncertainty and finding new meaning in life is an ongoing process, full of challenges and opportunities. It's crucial to remember that every step we take brings us closer to that more authentic and fulfilled version of ourselves.

In the final stretch of this exploration, I remind you that the path forward may seem bewildering at times, but it's filled with exciting and transformative possibilities. It's a journey of constant self-discovery, where every experience, even the most difficult ones, can become a springboard for personal growth.

Resilience or strength is also an invaluable tool in this journey of introspection. It's not just about overcoming challenges, but about learning from them and using those lessons to strengthen our determination and our will to move forward. Additionally, I want to emphasize the importance of maintaining an open and receptive mindset. Often, the answers we seek are not found in the destination, but in the process of searching and exploring. By allowing ourselves to be open to new experiences and perspectives, we can discover unexpected surprises that enrich our journey.

Finally, I remind you that this path forward is not just individual but intertwined with the journey of those around us. Finding new meaning in life can have a positive impact not only on ourselves but also on our relationships and communities.

In summary, as humans prepare to take the next step in our journey, we discover that the path forward is filled with endless possibilities. Each day brings us the opportunity to renew ourselves, grow, and find new meaning in life.

CHAPTER SEVEN

Revelation and Rebirth

"Love is the primary and highest goal to which a man can aspire." -
Viktor Frankl

After ending my second marriage, I spent several months deeply involved in church activities and not romantically involved with anyone, taking sacraments, attending Mass, praying daily, without committing to any ministry, but analyzing, studying, and learning about a life beyond this one, in my Creator, in my contribution to humanity... One day, I woke up around nine in the morning, and a word started repeating itself in my mind, saying: "Jeremiah... Jeremiah... Jeremiah...". The strange thing is that I was awake, I mean, no, it wasn't a dream. It wasn't a voice but a word inside my head saying "Jeremiah". I know it's a book in the Bible, but I've never been one to memorize the books, paragraphs, and verses of the Bible.

I asked myself:

-Where did that word come from?

-Could it be that God is trying to tell me something? Jeremiah is a very large book...

-I asked myself, Jeremiah what?

-"16" my own thought told me.

-Jeremiah 16.

I spent a couple of hours with doubt... and I went to search in my Bible what Jeremiah 16 says.

Do you know what it says? **"Do not take a wife or husband.... or have children in this place... for the Lord is angry and will destroy them"**!

That's indeed a strong message that can be quite intimidating. I had been asking God to show me which path to take, whether He wants me to marry again or if I should forget about it altogether. Throughout my life, I've felt that I lacked having a permanent partner, something that I, by my own will, postponed for years: having a traditional family life. I did it partly because I didn't want to owe anything to anyone, partly because I wanted to finish my career, because I love independence, and partly because the idea of self-sufficiency has always been ingrained in me. However, at this point in my life, a family with a husband and two dogs wouldn't be a bad thing, although I also feel fine being alone.

The thing is, the Lord was answering me.

A few days passed, and I told your uncle Julian, the most religious one in the family, and he said:

"Ah! But God, when He wants to give you a message, usually gives it to you twice, because He confirms to you what He tells you."

It's good to know. So, I went to my confessor and posed my doubt to him: "... I don't know if it's the enemy simply not wanting me to be happy with a husband."

The priest replied, "I don't believe the enemy would prompt you to read the Bible; that was a tremendous revelation!"

It's true that being alone is one thing and feeling alone is another. Right now, I'm in that struggle because besides that, I went to read more about Jeremiah 16, which I must finish reading, but I'm afraid the Lord might ask more of me. But I went to read a little more, and the message or interpretation that the Church gives to that chapter of the

Bible is that God was asking Jeremiah, yes, to pray a lot for his fellow beings, but He was also asking him for celibacy. Then I thought that I was focusing too much on myself, that I must ask for more, not only for God to guide me, but for God to guide everyone around me, to be better people and seek Him more.

In other words, evangelizing more, even though I've never been good at the gift of speech or making new friends or going to preach in a crowded square full of people I don't know.

Patty:

"You can start by evangelizing yourself, before evangelizing others."

Mónica:

"This means working on myself before trying to teach others."

Part of the interpretation of the book of Jeremiah 16 is that God asks for celibacy, as I mentioned before. So, I've always had issues with commitment. I barely mustered the courage to give a bit of my freedom in those two failed marriages, and now you're asking me for a commitment to celibacy? I asked. I've always been bad at committing because, even with God, I have that fear, so I felt frozen.

Patty:

So, that's what you need to work on. That's a new goal and a new purpose in life. Eureka!

I admire people who aren't afraid of commitment. I imagine that God must give them special gifts to be fully committed individuals from the start, although I believe that for most ordinary people, it's a struggle every day.

Mónica:

Patty helped me realize that we can start with a drop, that I don't need to be a full stream of water right away. It's better to be a constant drop than a stream of water that drowns and then it's over, it seemed like a good analogy to me. Everyone has the grace to be a drop of purity, that's the effort the Lord wants us to make. The church preaches that God wants us all to be saints. I never thought I'd become a saint, I think it's a bit arrogant to say, "I want to be holy," a bit naive. It seems to me that I've had the wrong vision of what it means to be holy.

Patty:

God wants us all to be saints. Now, considering the times we're in, where everything seems chaotic out there, we need to pray a lot and revisit the definition of what it means to 'be holy.'

Mónica:

I ask God a lot to enlighten me on how to share His word and at least for my nieces and nephews, my small circle of young people, to draw closer to God because they want nothing to do with God, nothing to do with religion. They judge the church very harshly.

Patty:

Perhaps that's exactly where the Lord wants you to be.

Mónica:

But how do I get these young ones to listen to me? Patty's words resonate with me and remind me that prayer may seem passive, but it's powerful. It's the most powerful thing we can do. If we can't do anything else for someone, it's the best we can offer for that person, instead of trying to persuade or convince them. If we kneel and pray, I can assure you that the Lord will intervene in some way. I also believe that we're living in times of the Parousia, and it's regrettable that the church doesn't proclaim it more, as it's a way to prepare people to realize how distant humanity is from God. There's a great lack of faith and love towards God and towards our fellow beings.

Patty:

Governments are excluding God from the equation, which leads to the idea that if He's not present, I can do whatever I want. This is a desire to please halfheartedly. Do you know what many hospitals and clinics did in some countries? They removed all the crucifixes! All to please groups that feel offended or believe they're obligated to follow a certain faith.

Mónica:

If you ask them, many no longer believe in God. No one thinks about their death because it's an unpleasant topic, much less do we think about divine judgment, without realizing that by closing our ears, we miss out on savoring the hope of salvation and eternal happiness right now. This is the goal of human beings, our true purpose for existing as humans.

So, my dear Genesis, let's reflect on how God calls people in different ways. Some are called through marriage, others through celibacy, and others through being single parents.

The important thing is not only the commitment we make but how we make that commitment.

Probably, at this point in my life, God wants me in a state of purity as part of my commitment. I believe that the Lord speaks to us and gives us the grace to live in that state of purity.

Génesis:

How do you receive this revelation? With fear, joy, hope, or as a requirement for your salvation.

Mónica:

Initially, with fear of commitment. Finally, I am receiving it with the joy of knowing that God has truly manifested and accepts my commitment to give Him whatever I can, each day, one step at a time. I don't have to sign a contract for eternity; I can renew that contract periodically or every day when I wake up. That's how I manage to overcome the fear of commitment.

And that is how I concluded that from now on, He will be my boyfriend, the love and center of my life.

Before we conclude this conversation, I want to thank you, Génesis, for listening to me and helping me find new goals that give meaning to my life. First, to seek reconciliation with those whom I may have offended; second, to ask God for the gift of speech to evangelize those who want to hear about His love and justice; and third, to live each day with a new goal, offering Him a drop of purity until the day He sends me a new revelation or calls me back home. Waking up every morning with these thoughts gives a new meaning to my life.

Come here, Genesis! Give me a liberating hug, my beloved inner child!

EPILOGUE

Mónica discovers that the best refuge is within herself and accompanies her wherever she goes, manifesting itself primarily when she is in an environment where love is reciprocal: whether it's in self-love, accepting herself as she is, in the extended family, in close friends, or in her religious community.

She also comes to understand that legacies are not exclusively negative; there are positive aspects to them, and each of us is the result of that mix. She recognizes the importance of focusing on the positive aspects. For Mónica, who describes herself as a strong, independent, hardworking, entrepreneurial, and protective woman of her loved ones, she understands that her achievements in life are the result of a combination of inherited or learned virtues, as well as her own efforts. This is her personal definition of success.

Finally, Monica finds herself facing three possibilities: 1) being open to a relationship with the prospect of a dedicated marriage; 2) considering a dedicated religious life; 3) opting for a life of voluntary celibacy, and possibly even a fourth option: that of raising a child as a single mother. After deep reflection, she concludes that the purity of the body should not be a commitment imposed by the lack of alternatives, but a conscious choice that gives meaning to her gift. As indicated in the New Covenant (Hebrews 8, Jesus is the true Sacrifice) among Christians, just as in the times of Jeremiah, marriage and motherhood are still honored, however, the New Testament honors singles, telling them to consider their natural state as a call from God as in the case of Jeremiah (es.enduringword.com).

Mónica concludes and adjusts to a reality she didn't expect, shifting away from her extremist, black-and-white thinking represented by marriage or religious life, and adopts a mindset of flexible thinking to find a version of commitment that aligns more with her nature, opting for a gray area represented in the decision to take her sexuality and commitment one day at a time.

Mónica also acknowledges that her personal examination reveals unfinished tasks, such as accepting the skeletons in the closet she had previously avoided, such as continuing her process of healing from childhood abuse through cognitive transformative therapy to change her feelings of guilt towards her mother. She recognizes the need to forgive her father's mistress, whose existence she had previously denied, and overcome resentments towards her older half-siblings, who seemed to have unfairly and uniquely benefited from her father's inheritance.

Only after this period of self-evaluation and her commitment to addressing unfinished tasks can Mónica confidently continue towards the next stage of her journey, renewed in soul and purpose.

THE END

REFERENCES:

- Frankl, Viktor, "Man in Search of Life's meaning" - *"El Hombre en Busca del Sentido",* 1946
- Holy Latin-American Bible, International Catholic Society – Rome, 1972
- Jeremiah 16: es.enduringword.com
- Powel, John, "Love Comes from Within", S.J. 1989. www.RCL.Benziger.com
- Zambrano, Byron, "Man in Search of Life's Meaning" (*"El Hombre en Busca del Sentido de la Vida"*), Master Audio Book. 3ª. Edition.
- Father Carlos Casado, Podcast en YouTube.
- 2024 Life.Church. YouVersion. https://www.bible.com/es-ES/bible/210/PRO.31.10-31.BLP

ACKNOWLEDGEMENTS:

- Rengil, Marco Antonio, and Lazo, Marisa - podcast 132. YouTube

- Rengil, Marco Antonio, "Accepting Yourself" *("Aceptándote a ti mismo")*. YouTube Podcast.
- Rojas Estape, Marian, "I also Had Mental Health Problems" *("Yo También Tenía Problemas de Salud Mental"),* Podcast en YouTube
- One Percent Better – Animated Book Summary, YouTube

Made in United States
North Haven, CT
02 July 2025